The Adventures Of Veda & Dino

Shweta Korde

BookLeaf Publishing

India | USA | UK

Made with ❤ on the BookLeaf Publishing Platform
www.bookleafpub.in
www.bookleafpub.com

Dedication

To **Veda**—

my brightest light, my wildest dream,

whose wonder echoes in every line.

To **Dino**—

our golden-hearted explorer,

who taught me the joy of walking beside.

To **Amit**—

for your quiet faith, steady strength,

and for holding space when my stories ran wild.

And to **Mom**—

who gave me the roots to imagine,

and the wings to believe.

Preface

This book began with **Veda**—my daughter, my wonder.
Her questions, courage, and wild joy made me want to
capture something lasting.

And always beside her—**Dino**, our golden retriever and
gentle explorer. Though he's no longer with us, he lives
on in these pages, still running, still glowing.

These poems are about more than adventure. They're
about listening, sharing, and finding your way home—
with kindness as your compass.

For the child curled up close.
For the grown-up chasing wonder.
For those who remember. And those still becoming.

Thank you for stepping into this world with us.
You've already found the first glow.

With love,
Shweta

Acknowledgements

To the friends who encouraged me—often without
realizing—
thank you for holding space when it mattered most.

To the artists and storytellers who remind me that
wonder has weight.

To quiet mornings, strong coffee, and fleeting moments
where the world grew still enough to write.

And to the part of me that still believes in firefly songs
and secret maps—thank you for staying

"Where Tides Tell Their Tale:

The Beginning of the Beach Adventures"

One bright morning by the sea,
Veda and Dino ran wild and free.
Where waves whispered and tide pools gleamed,
They stepped into a world once dreamed.

A curious crab, a silver light,
Led them through coral caves in flight.
With mermaids, shells, and secrets deep,
They found the truths the oceans keep.

Now through these poems, journey wide —
Where kindness flows with every tide.

Poem 1: The Moon Pearl's Glow

Down by the shore on a soft golden night,
Veda and Dino saw something bright—
A pearl on the sand, glowing and round,
It shimmered and floated without a sound.

"Dino, come quick!" Veda gave a shout.
"Who lost this pearl? Let's figure it out!"
A mermaid named Marina swam near with a smile,
"That pearl holds magic—it's been lost a while."

Before they could guess who it was for,
A crab snatched it fast and ran to his shore.
"It's mine!" he snapped. "So shiny and grand—
A treasure like this belongs in my hand!"

"Wait," said Marina, "it's not just for show.
Its light keeps the balance. It's meant to flow."
But deep in his cave, the pearl went dim,
Its shimmer lost in the dark with him.

The tide grew tight, the waves pulled low,
A swirl of glowfish began to show.
"They've come for the pearl!" Marina cried,
"Their magic fades if it's kept inside."

The crab looked down—its shine was gone.
The glow had dulled. The gift withdrawn.
Veda stepped forward, calm and kind,
She placed the pearl where waves unwind.

The glowfish spun in silver flight,
Restoring the sea with gentle light.
The crab let go with one deep sigh—
"Some things are meant to swim, not lie."

The stars looked down, the ocean sang,
The pearl returned to where it sprang.
Not all treasures are meant to keep—
Some glow brightest in the deep.

Veda's Little Thought:
"Some things shine more when we let them go."

Poem 2: The Ocean Festival & The Lonely Giant

Beneath the waves where lanterns swayed,
The ocean danced, the drums were played.
The Ocean Race was set to start—
With swirls and spins, each took their part.

Shadow Crab boasted, "I'll win again!"
And zipped through hoops with puffed-up grin.
But Dino paused—he heard a sound,
From coral caves below the ground.

A Giant Octopus, soft and shy,
Watched racers speed and swimmers fly.
"I don't belong," he gently said.
"I'm far too big." He dropped his head.

"Come join the fun!" said Veda's voice.
"The sea has room. You have a choice!"
He slowly moved, unsure, unsure...
But swam ahead with growing lure.

The race began, the dolphins flew,
Turtles twisted, jellyfish too.
Shadow Crab took a secret track—
But seaweed caught him, pulling back!

Dino barked and led the way,
"Veda, he's stuck! He went astray!"
The Octopus reached out with care,
And freed the crab still tangled there.

Shadow Crab blinked, a bit surprised—
The giant helped? The one he'd sized?
Back at the end, though last to land,
The crowd still clapped with heart and hand.

The Ocean King then gave a cheer,
"For kindness shown, you're champions here!"
The Giant smiled, his worry gone,
And joined the feast till early dawn.

Veda's Little Thought:
"Big or small, there's space for all."

Poem 3: The Bubble & the Manta's Song

A shimmer rose above the reef—
A glowing bubble, round and deep.
It pulsed with light, it held a tune,
And shimmered brighter with the moon.

No fin had touched it, none came near—
A memory stirred inside, unclear.
Veda swam with Dino, slow,
Drawn to its soft, unspoken glow.

Then through the tide came Luma, shy—
A manta ray with watchful eye.
She circled once, then settled low,
Still guarding what she couldn't show.

"Why hold it close?" young Veda said.
Luma replied with a gentle head:
"Some songs can stir what's tucked away—
The aches we hide, the fears we weigh."

Shadow Crab scoffed from below,
"A bubble's just a flashy show!"
But even he stayed still and stared,
At something glowing, softly shared.

Dino barked and turned his head
To coral caves where silence spread.
Behind a veil of shifting blue
Lay Sora—quiet, out of view.

She once danced bright in reef and spray,
But hurt her fin one stormy day.
She hadn't danced or leapt since then—
Afraid she'd never dance again.

Veda hummed a steady tune,
Dino twirled beneath the moon.
Sora stirred, then drifted near,
Drawn by kindness, not just cheer.

Luma nodded, soft and slow,
Then touched the bubble's outer glow.
It shimmered once, then split the sea,
Unfolding song and memory.

The reef lit up, the current twirled—
And Sora stretched, then softly swirled.
Her fin still ached—but in that light,
She danced again, not out of fright.

Shadow Crab, with nothing to prove,
Left behind a shell—a gentle move.
Not taken this time, but placed with care—
A quiet gift, just resting there.

Veda smiled, and Dino spun—
Not to fix her, just to have fun.
The reef had room for every part—
And slowly, so did Sora's heart.

Veda's Little Thought:
*"We don't have to be all healed to shine—
Just brave enough to try in time."*

"Veda & Dino in the Land of Sand"

One golden dawn, with skies aglow,
Veda and Dino wandered slow.
Beyond the shore, past hills of sand,
They found the desert's dreaming land.

The dunes, they whispered soft and wide,
Of stories buried deep inside.
With every step, the silence grew—
And magic stirred where warm winds blew.

A beetle spoke in riddled rhyme,
A camel marched to ancient time.
A tortoise taught them how to wait,
While stars revealed the desert's fate.

These poems rise like desert flame,
Each tale unique, yet all the same—
Of wonder found and truths set free,
In shifting sands and mystery.

Poem 4: The Whistling Dunes & the Lost Camel

The dunes rolled high, the sun beat low,
Veda and Dino moved with the flow.
The Whistling Wind spun all around—
A dancing riddle, a twisting sound.

From the sand came a flurry and thud—
Zazu the camel, splashed with mud!
"I raced too far," he puffed with pride,
"But now I'm lost, with no guide."

The dunes had shifted, trails erased.
"We'll help," said Veda, slowing her pace.
"Let's follow the wind—it might just know
Which way the gentler footsteps go."

But Zazu dashed with stubborn cheer,
"I'll lead the way—the path is clear!"
Yet every turn led back again,
The dunes repeating, just the same.

Dino barked from a gentle rise—
Three beetles danced, small and wise.
"We're Bop, Boppi, and Bloop," they said,
"The desert listens to your tread."

They rolled their glowing orbs in time,
Marking rhythm, step, and line.
"Too fast," said Bloop, "and paths will hide—
But walk with care, and dunes will guide."

Zazu paused and matched their beat.
A buried stone rose at his feet.
A glowing glyph began to shine—
The desert's way, by calm design.

Veda smiled, the wind grew still.
The dunes aligned with quiet will.
Zazu grinned, his pride made small—
"Turns out slow was best of all."

Veda's Little Thought:
"Rush, and the trail turns unclear—
Walk gently, and the way appears."

Poem 5: The Mirage Garden & the Keeper of Truth

Through heat and haze, they wandered on,
Till shimmering flowers softly shone.
A garden bloomed where none should grow—
Mirage or magic? They didn't know.

Veda stepped in with wondering eyes,
And reached for a bloom shaped like the skies.
Snap! went the stem—then silence fell,
The garden dimmed beneath a spell.

Tufan appeared, steady and slow,
A tortoise wise, with eyes that know.
"These blooms respond to hearts that shine,
But fade when truth steps out of line."

"I didn't pick it!" Veda lied.
But Dino barked and turned aside.
He dropped his ears, then gave a sigh,
And placed the flower by her side.

The petals drooped, the color fled—
As if the truth had softly bled.
Veda looked down, then breathed in deep,
"I did... I picked it. I didn't mean to keep."

From shadowed stone, a shimmer blue—
Sola the Scorpion slid into view.
She circled once, then gave a tap—
A golden glow rose from Veda's lap.

"Sola helps the truth shine bright.
Her sting brings out what feels just right."
The garden stirred, the blooms returned,
A softened breeze, a lesson learned.

Tufan said, "The desert keeps
Its secrets where the silence sleeps.
But when truth walks with open eyes,
The dunes reveal their ancient ties."

Sola turned, her tail aglow,
And traced a path in sand below.
"Let's follow it," Veda said,
As stars lit up the trail ahead.

Dino wagged and took the lead,
The trail ahead was wide and deep.
The desert opened, calm and wide—
With ancient secrets tucked inside.

Veda's Little Thought:
"Even a small truth can help the world bloom again."

Poem 6: The Compass of the Sun

Veda and Dino stepped inside,
A cave of stone, tall, dark, and wide.
The wind was gone, the world was still—
The air around gave both a chill.

Strange shapes and signs glowed on the floor,
A puzzle map and something more.
Dino barked and gave a spin,
As if the answer lay within.

Sola tapped a glowing square—
But nothing moved in temple air.
The **Beetles** rolled their orbs around,
But couldn't match the desert's sound.

"Try the rhythm," Bloop said low,
"The quiet song the dunes still know."
Veda stepped with steady pace,
And lit a path across the space.

The compass rose with golden light,
Its glow grew warm, its circle bright.
It didn't point to far-off land—
But shone right near where they did stand.

Zazu's prints were on the sand,
Just outside—like a guiding hand.
Veda smiled, her heart beat light,
"The desert knows when we get it right."

Then something stirred in skies above,
A golden bird with wings of love.
Navi soared through glowing red,
And gently circled overhead.

They didn't race, they didn't run—
The compass glowed with who they'd become.

**Dino stepped forward, sure and bright,
His paws aglow in starlit light.
The path ahead stretched deep and wide—
With ancient secrets tucked inside.**

Veda's Little Thought:
"Sometimes, you don't need to know the way.
You just need to feel where you belong."

"Into the Green: The Forest Adventure Begins"

Through swaying vines and emerald light,
Veda and Dino stepped into night.
The jungle sang in rustling tones,
Of hidden trails and ancient stones.

A pixie giggled from mossy ground,
As fireflies twirled without a sound.
A brownie bold, a gnome so wise,
Revealed the forest's soft disguise.

Each path they walk, a story bright,
Of courage, trust, and forest light.
Now poems grow where shadows play—
Come join their wild, enchanted way.

Poem 7: "The Canopy Crown & the Pixie's Tune"

At jungle's edge, where fireflies play,
Veda and Dino skipped their way.
But something felt a little wrong—
The trees were quiet, not full of song.

The flowers drooped, the colors pale,
The jungle breeze had lost its tale.
And high above, in twisted vines,
A leafy crown had lost its shine.

Then fluttering down from a mossy bloom,
Came Mira the Leafling, glowing with gloom.
Her leafy shoulders drooped with care,
"The music's gone. It's quiet... there."

A tiny sprite with a leafy cape,
Hair like twigs in a mushroom shape.
"Oh dear," she sighed, "the crown's held tight,
The vines won't drop it, not without light.

The Jungle Music Box plays their tune—
But it needs a key to hum and bloom!"

Just then, patter pat, came feet on the ground—
Veda peeked out, hearing the sound.
"What's going on?" she asked with care,
As Dino gave a sniffy stare.

Mira looked up with teary eyes,
"A tricksy pixie took our prize!
The winding key is gone today—
Pipnut the Pixie zipped away."

"Don't worry," said Veda, "we'll find your key.
Come on, Dino, let's search the trees!"
She listened close—a giggle!—a pop!
A glitter trail looped through the treetop.

"Did someone call?" a voice rang clear—
And Pipnut spun with a cheeky cheer.
He danced in air, then zipped from sight,
"Come find me if you want it right!"

Through bouncing ferns and ticklish grass,
Dino gave chase—a leafy splash!
He leapt through vines, he sniffed and spun,

But Pipnut laughed, "You call this fun?"

Suddenly—*snag!*—a vine curled tight,
Caught the pixie mid-flight!
"I'm stuck!" he gasped. "They want a tune—
A song that's silly, like a baboon!"

Veda clapped and grabbed two leaves,
She swayed her hips and tapped her knees.
**"Jungle wiggle, honey bee,
Dino dances, one-two-three!"**

The vines all shook with a leafy cheer,
And gently set Pipnut down near.
"Well played!" he giggled, "You win today—
Here's your key. Now play away!"

Pipnut chuckled, light as mist,
"Next time, the clue will come with a twist!"
He blew a kiss, then zipped from view,
In a trail of sparkles and jungle dew.

Veda turned the key just right,
The box sang out in golden light.
The vines let go with swaying cheer,
And brought the crown down soft and near.

Drums thumped low from roots below,
And fireflies spun in golden glow.
Birds burst out with joyful calls—
Color climbed the mossy walls.

And as the trees began to sway,
The jungle bloomed in bright display.

Veda's Little Thought:
"Some doors don't open with keys at all—
Just laughter and a leafy call."

Poem 8: The Inkfruit Grove & the Drawing Vines

At the heart of the jungle, past mossy green,
Veda and Dino found a place unseen—
Where vines grew wild in twisty loops,
And berries hung low in inky swoops.

"Look!" cried Pipnut with glittery cheer,
"These fruits can draw things out of thin air!"
He squished a berry, gave it a swirl—
And sketched midair a dancing squirrel.

Veda gasped as it sprang to life,
Twisting and twirling in jiggly strife.
She drew a kite with a giggly face—
While Dino doodled a cake to chase!

It puffed up high with frosting bright—
A wobbly mountain of chocolate delight.
Dino leapt with frosting nose,
As jelly bounced between his toes.

Ink-bunnies bounced, and hats flew high,
A flying spoon zipped through the sky!
The vines around began to twitch—
And tangled Pipnut in a laughing stitch.

"Oops!" Pipnut giggled, "It's getting wild!"
Veda looked up and gently smiled.
"The grove's too full, it's losing track—
Let's help it breathe and bring it back."

She took a breath and stilled her hand,
Then sketched a door with leafy strands.
A glowing path began to grow—
Lit by the vines in a soft green glow.

The doodles paused and waved goodbye,
Like dreams dissolving in the sky.
Dino barked, then gave a grin,
As peace returned to vine and limb.

The grove exhaled, serene and still—
The buzzing leaves grew soft and chill.
Pipnut smiled with berry-stained hands,
"That was better than I had planned!"

Veda laughed, "Next time, let's draw with care—
Because magic listens to what we share."

Veda's Little Thought:
*"Magic is fun when it's drawn with heart—
Imagination is a kind of art."*

Poem 9: Dino's Nose Knows

Sniff-sniff-snuffle... what's that smell?
Not flowers, fruit, or Fernabelle.
It smells like giggles lost midair—
Like magic fading, unaware.

Veda draws a moon so high,
Pipnut zips and doodles by.
But I don't wag—I twitch instead.
Something's wrong near Flowerbed.

I sniff through vines, I leap a log,
Then bounce—*boing!*—on a mossy frog!
Milo the Mossbouncer wobbles wide,
"Too much magic is hard to hide.

Pipnut's doodles danced too far—
Their silly smells confused the air.
Now jungle lights don't sparkle fair."

I nudge ahead with sniffy grace,

Past drooping vines that lost their place.
Above me blinks two giant eyes—
Tulla the Tarsier, quiet and wise.

"The Scent Spirit's stuck," she softly said,
"Too many smells—it's gone to bed."
I sniff the hush—a golden glow,
Curled where sleepy bushes grow.

So I do what Dinos do best—
I roll, I bark, I wiggle and jest!
I chase my tail, I leap at light—
And sparkles rise in swirling flight.

A shimmer lifts, gold and free—
The Spirit twirls and hums at me.
Not flying cake or doodled flair—
But Dino-joy cleared up the air.

Veda laughs and Pipnut cheers,
Milo boings and Tulla peers.
The jungle sways with gentle breeze,
And magic hums through blooming trees.

Dino's Little Thought:
*"A pixie's mess may cloud the air—
But joy and play can clear despair."*

Poem 10: The Firefly Festival & the Jungle Jamboree

The jungle buzzed in golden gleam,
The trees aglow, a leafy dream.
Veda and Dino twirled with glee—
Tonight was the Firefly Jubilee!

The fireflies lit the skies so high,
Their wings a shimmer in the sky.
Each creature brought a spark, a tune,
To help the jungle hum and bloom.

♪ *Boom-ta-ta!* went Milo's feet—
A mossy drum with bouncing beat.
Pipnut zipped in zigzag spins,
His trail went *zing!* on leafy skins.
Mira twirled in glowing rings,
As flutes hummed soft on vine-strung strings.

But near the edge, beneath a tree,
Sori sat in secrecy.

She knew the rhythms, every tone—
But always felt she danced alone.

Dino barked and spun in place,
His waggy tail a wiggly bass.
Sori laughed—*flash!* her hues—
A swirl of soft and glowing blues.

Blink-blink-blink! the fireflies flew,
Their rhythm rising, fresh and new.
Veda smiled, "Come join the bliss—
You're part of all the joy in this!"

Then came a *pop!*—a bubbling beat!
Noko the frog sprang to his feet.
"My bubbles bounce when I feel shy..."
Sori said, "That's music—give it a try!"

But Pipnut twirled and tried to boast—
Poof! a bubble caught him most!
"Whoa!" he yelped, now floating high—
Dino barked and danced nearby.

The jungle thumped in snap-snap snaps,
While fireflies spun in click-clack claps.
Noko's bubbles bobbed and gleamed,
While Sori's colors gently streamed.

Then Pipnut landed—*boof!*—on Milo's rear,
And laughter burst in leafy cheer.
No perfect step, no need to lead—
Just hearts that danced at joy's own speed.

The jungle sighed with glowing ease,
Its music drifting through the trees.
A crown unseen beneath the ground—
Where rhythm lives without a sound.

Veda's Little Thought:
"Every laugh, every bounce, every beat you bring—
Adds music to the jungle's swing."

Veda & Dino's Snowlight Tales

Snowflakes fall and everything hushes.
Veda and Dino step into a land of frost and wonder.
Here, the wind tells secrets,
The moon puts on a circus,
And a crown sleeps deep beneath the ice.
But even in a world made of snow,
Big choices wait.
This is Veda's last adventure—
Where she'll face what it means to be strong,
To be kind,
And to let go when it matters most.
Because real magic isn't just what you find—
It's what you're willing to give back.

Poem 11: The Snow Circus & the Missing Moon

The world was still. The wind turned thin.
Snowflakes danced on Veda's skin.
The trees wore coats of softest white—
And stars blinked low, not high, that night.

Veda and Dino climbed a hill,
Their breath a puff, the world so still.
They didn't know what they might see—
Just followed trails of mystery.

Beyond the pines, a glowing sign:
"Tonight Only — Snow Circus Time!"
Lights spun wild in icy cheer—
The snowy show was drawing near.

A juggler flipped through frosty air:
"I'm Nimbus! Welcome! Look up there!"
He tossed three stars with sparkling ease
And vanished in a swirl of breeze.

The snow lit up in rings and spins—
Tents and stars and violin strings.
Dino barked and chased a star,
Sliding, spinning near and far.

A golden firefly zipped by—
"I'm Trixel!" said the glow in sky.
She looped and laughed, then twirled with glee.
Veda beamed and danced carefree.

"Step in the spotlight!" someone cried.
She danced as snowflakes spun and sighed.
She tossed one high into the blue—
And all the world felt bright and new.

But then the music faded slow.
The moon above refused to go.

Nimbus gasped and looked around—
"The moon won't budge—it loves the light!"
It loves the joy, the dance ,
something's paused it here tonight."

Trixel flew down, soft and kind:
"Some magic stays when joy won't glide.
The moon's just waiting for a sign—

To know it's time to rise and shine."

Dino nudged Veda, sweet and small,
Then gave a bark that said it all.
Veda smiled, then spun once more—
And slowly stepped beyond the floor.

The moon rose up, its silver free.
The stars returned in twos and three.
The tents all faded, hush came near—
As frostflakes danced in gentle cheer.

Nimbus bowed, Trixel flew.
Dino wagged a soft thank-you.
Veda grinned, her heart aglow—
Not from the show, but letting go.

Veda's Little Thought:
*"The best kind of magic isn't mine—
It's what I give back when it's time."*

Poem 12: The Crystal Crown & the Frozen Choice

The circus tents had gone to mist,
Snowflakes shimmered, swirled, and kissed.

Veda and Dino walked uphill,
Past icy stones and caves so still.
They found a chamber deep and wide,
With crystals growing side to side.
And right up front on frozen stone—
A shining crown sat all alone.

She touched it once—it felt like snow,
But soft and warm with gentle glow.
She placed it gently on her head...
And snowflakes swirled around instead!
She raised her hand—*whoosh!* snow took flight!
It swooped in rings of dancing light.
"Whoa!" she laughed, "The snow knows me!"
The crown had set her magic free!
She built a slide, a snowflake swing—

A glitter path, a snowy ring.
She made the winds slow down, then spin—
A little world she held within.

But then—the bunny froze mid-hop.
The swirling flakes began to stop.
The snow hung heavy, pale and tight—
The cold grew sharp. It lost its light.
Dino's wag slowed down to none—
The cave forgot how fun was fun.

She turned around and blinked with care—
And saw a shimmer in the air.
A crab appeared in silver snow,
Not real, but soft, and faintly aglow.
He didn't speak or wave or cry,
Just gave a glance and wandered by.
Then placed some tiny things with care—
A ribbon, shell, and silver hair.
She knew his shape, his quiet way—
The Shadow Crab who once took light to play.
Now here he was, not hoarding more—
Just letting treasures touch the floor.

Then came a voice both soft and kind,
A whisper floating through her mind:
"The ocean gave, and so can snow—

Magic flows when you let go."
The bunny blinked and turned to glide,
Its tiny footprints side by side.
Dino gave a hopeful bark—
And Veda felt a warming spark.

She took the crown down from her head,
And gave it back with care instead.
The snowflakes danced, the winds returned—
And every icy crystal turned.
Dino barked and wagged again,
The snow was soft, the chill felt friend.
The bunny spun and bounced in cheer—
The crown had never made that clear.

Veda's Little Thought:
"Magic's not just mine to steer—
Sometimes it's best to let it clear."

Poem 13: Flicker & the Fire That Stayed

Veda and Dino walked through snow,
Their pace was soft, their steps were slow.
So much they'd seen, so much they'd done—
Now even dreams weighed like the sun.

They found a log, all dry and deep,
Lit a small fire, curled up for sleep.
Dino yawned and licked her hand—
While stars blinked over snowy land.

But just as Veda closed one eye,
A flicker danced across the sky.
It dipped, then wobbled—dim and small—
A golden bird about to fall.

Her feathers sparked, then blinked out slow.
She chirped, "I lost my flying glow."
"I'm Flicker. I was late," she said,
Her little flame a thread of red.

"I thought the circle came and went—
And I'd just missed the warm it meant."
Veda smiled, "You're right on time.
The fire stays for every light."

She scooched aside and made some space—
A quiet, glowy, welcome place.
Dino stretched with one big sigh,
Then curled beneath the starlit sky.

Flicker blinked and fluttered near—
Still shy, but held by those right here.
One by one, the circle grew—
Not for show, but something true.

Trixel looped a steady light,
And Flare made room with gentle might.
Nimbus tossed a spark that stayed—
No spell, no speech, just care displayed.

Veda yawned, her cheeks aglow,
And nestled gently in the snow.
Dino snuggled close once more—
Their journey echoing at the core.

The final fire, calm and deep,
Held every promise they would keep.
No roaring blaze, no wild cheer—
Just love that warmed the ones most near.

Veda's Little Thought:
"You don't need magic loud or bright—
Just quiet hearts to keep a light."

The Map Inside: Where the Adventures Rest

The fire was low, its crackle sweet,
With glowing ash and drowsy heat.
Around its light in quiet rows,
Lay sleeping bags like curling toes.

The tents stood zipped in moonlight's care,
While stars hung still in frosted air.
Veda stirred and blinked one eye—
The night was soft, the fire low-dry.

Dino yawned and stretched his toes,
Then wriggled close beneath her nose.
She rubbed her eyes—and saw it there:
A moon pearl nestled by her hair.

A jungle vine, half-tied in thread,
Was looped around her sleeping bed.
No one stirred. The world stayed slow—
But something sparkled in the glow.

Dino blinked and gave a grin.
She touched the pearl and tucked it in.
They didn't speak. They didn't need—
The magic answered every deed.

She thought of waves and golden sand,
Of shifting dunes and crabby hands,
Of forest songs and snowy skies—
And how they danced, and dared, and tried.

No shiny trophies by her side.
Just stories she could feel inside.
And something steady in her chest—
A glowing calm, a quiet rest.

She smiled, then let her eyelids fall,
The fire's glow now soft and small.
The sky grew light, the stars withdrew—
And she whispered, "Maybe... it was true."

Veda's Final Thought:
"I don't need maps to roam or ride—
The truest treasure lives inside."

Veda and Dino's Magical Friends

Main Characters

Veda

A curious, kind-hearted, and brave little girl. Veda sees the world with wonder, asks questions no one else thinks to ask, and often becomes the heart of the journey. Her strength lies in listening, sharing, and leading with empathy.

Dino

A loyal, playful golden retriever and Veda's best friend. Dino is brave, affectionate, and often intuitive—his nose, paws, and gentle instincts help guide Veda through sticky or magical situations. Though he doesn't speak, his presence speaks volumes.

1. Beach Series Characters

- **The Moon Pearl**- A mystical glowing pearl representing balance, kindness, and letting go. It appears in both the first beach poem and again in the Snow series.
- **Marina the Mermaid**- A gentle and graceful sea-dweller who introduces Veda and Dino to the magical world beneath the tide. She guides without controlling, and embodies calm, curiosity, and trust.
- **Shadow Crab** - Initially a mischievous hoarder of shiny things, Shadow Crab undergoes a meaningful transformation—learning about sharing, balance, and responsibility. He returns in the Snow series as a memory or imagined figure to help Veda reflect on her own choices.
- **Sea Butterfly-** A glowing, graceful sea creature who serves as a spiritual guide—offering silent wisdom and luminous direction.
- **Baby Sea Dragon** - A young, glowing creature who loses his guiding shell and needs help to restore his light. Represents vulnerability, dependence, and eventual restoration.
- **Magical Glowfish-** A school of shimmering, luminous fish who help light the way during underwater journeys.

- **Wise Sea Turtle-** An ancient, glowing turtle full of ocean wisdom and gentle humor. Moves slowly but sees deeply.
- **The Lonely Giant-** A giant sea being, gentle and misunderstood, who wants to join the Ocean Festival but doesn't know how. Learns inclusion and joyful presence.
- **Playful Manta Ray (Sora & Luma)-** Two joyful rays who help guide Veda and Dino during the memory-restoring journey in the final beach poem.

2. Desert Series Characters

- **The Sand Spirit-** A mystical presence that speaks in riddles and metaphors. It tests Veda and Dino's patience, stillness, and intuition.
- **Kimo the Young Camel-** Proud but uncertain, Kimo is searching for his own path and learns that being heard sometimes begins with listening.
- **Zahar the Jackal-** Clever, tricky, and prideful at first. Zahar tries to outwit others but later realizes the value of honesty and redemption. Evolves meaningfully across the arc.
- **Old Desert Tortoise-** Slow-moving, deeply wise, and full of warm riddles. Helps Veda understand patience and inner clarity.

3. Jungle Series Characters

- **Mira the Leafling-** A tiny, glowing jungle sprite with twiggy hair and a leafy cape. Gentle and worried. Acts as the emotional pulse of the jungle.
- **Pipnut the Pixie-** A mischievous, cheeky pixie who hides keys, teases, and tests Veda's patience. Learns about trust, rhythm, and friendship.
- **Sori the Jungle Sprite-** A magical vine-doodler who expresses herself through living art. Sensitive, creative, and emotionally intuitive.
- **Milo the Jungle Elephant-** Shy, kind, and a little clumsy. Loves watching things from the sidelines until invited to join.
- **Tulle the Tarsier** *(brief appearance)-* A small, wide-eyed creature who lives in the scent-sheltering tree. Represents the quiet keepers of forgotten magic.
- **Noko the Bubble Frog-** A bashful frog who creates glowing bubble shows but lacks confidence. Finds his moment at the Firefly Festival.
- **Sori's Brother (Unnamed Chameleon)-** Appears as a background helper during the festival—a rainbow-shifting chameleon who quietly supports the show.

- **Fireflies-** Glowing jungle spirits of joy and light. They represent the rhythm, energy, and celebration of belonging.

4. Snow Series Characters

- **Nimbus the Snow Juggler-** A cheerful snow-being who juggles moonlight and guides Veda through the magical snow circus.
- **Trixel the Firefly in a Snow Globe-** Tiny, glowing, and full of wisdom. Lives in a snow globe lantern, offering warmth and direction.
- **Flare the Snow Bunny-** Silent and gentle, Flare watches over the crystal crown cave. A quiet guardian of balance.
- **The Ice Mirror-** A reflective magical object that shows what Veda could become if led by power alone. Represents internal reflection and choice.
- **Flicker the Glowbird-** A timid golden bird whose light goes out when she's alone. Her spark is restored through quiet friendship.